CW01211978

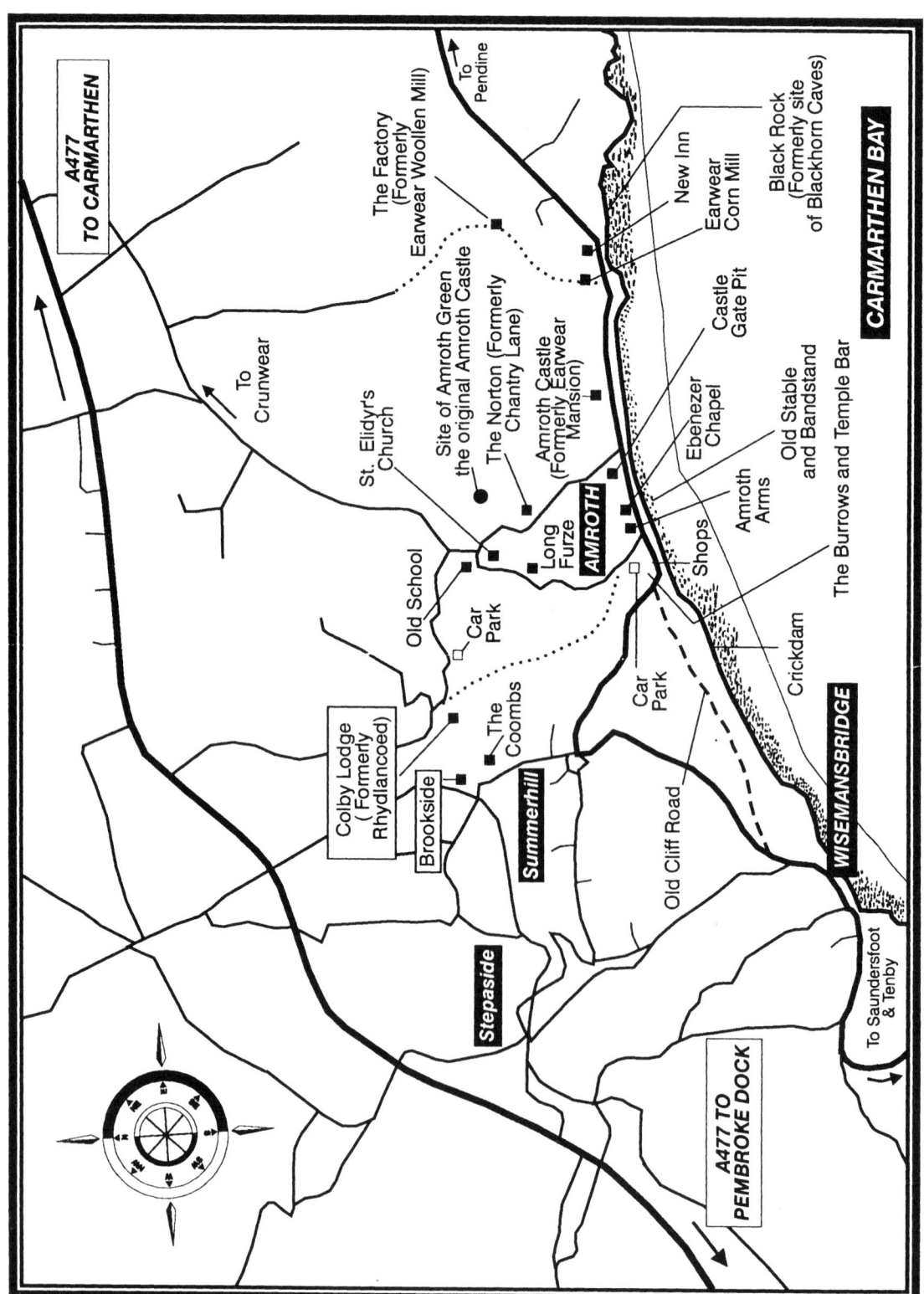

Map: Alan Shepherd

AMROTH

A Brief History

Roscoe Howells

GOMER

First Impression—2000

ISBN 1 85902 853 5

© Roscoe Howells

Roscoe Howells has asserted his right under the Copyright, Designs and Patents Act, 1988, to be identified as Author of this Work.

All rights reserved. No part of this book may be reproduced, stored in a retrieval system, or transmitted in any form or by any means, electronic, electrostatic, magnetic tape, mechanical, photocopying, recording or otherwise without permission in writing from the Author.

Printed in Wales at
Gomer Press, Llandysul, Ceredigion

To the staff at the Pembrokeshire Records Office,
for their friendship and patience over the years,
and for all their help which has so often been
far beyond the call of duty.

Introduction

This little book has been written in response to the requests of the many visitors who would like to know something of the history of Amroth.

It is far from being comprehensive, and seeks to do nothing more than mention a few of the highlights of the fascinating story of that which has gone before, all of which will be the subject of a far more detailed work currently in the process of preparation.

In expressing my thanks to the many who have helped in various ways I do not think that any of them will object if I mention by name only Gary Davies, for his great help with old pictures, and his grandmother, Mrs Eileen Algate, for sharing so many memories and old newspaper cuttings saved over the years by her mother, the late Mrs Winnie James. The roots of their family go deep into the soil of Amroth parish.

Not surprisingly, those who ask for a book on Amroth do so in the village shop. It is in response to this that this initial work has been prepared, and great thanks are due to the proprietors of the Osborne Shop, William and Susan Thwaites, for their initiative and financial support which have made it possible.

Finally, I would also say thank you to my good friend Byron Rogers, historian and distinguished journalist, for so readily agreeing to write the Foreword.

R.H. April 2000

Foreword

Mr Roscoe Howells could for all practical purposes be living on the hard shoulder of the M4. He lives in Amroth, a holiday village in West Wales, where in summer incurious strangers come, their sheer numbers treading down its history, its folklore, its sense of community, and where in winter the lights come on in a fraction of its houses. This is something he now seeks to redress. Before the ice-cream, before the sun-block factor 8, there was a village ….

A retired farmer, novelist and God's Own Nuisance, he has in his time sought to redress many things: the bone-headedness of councils, the arrogance of agricultural bureaucracy, the short-comings of large corporations. From Amroth, on a computer which he mastered in old age, and which in his hands is the equivalent of an assault rifle, the books and the letters get written.

To the managing director, Bowater Scott, 'Dear Sir, For longer and stronger than I can remember we have used nothing but Andrex lavatory paper. Yes, we have tried the odd roll of something else, but, wipe for wipe, Andrex beats them all. At least it did until recently. Whatever is this new rubbish you have substituted? Don't tell me you are now catering exclusively for the yobboes hurling your wares from the football terraces. Do you really sell that many to them you can afford to ignore the home market? Yours sincerely…' There are fat cats in Britain who award themselves pay rises at the mere mention of his name.

He is not a man of many doubts. He will believe until the day he dies that Bill Frost, a local carpenter, was the first man to fly, eight years before the Wright Brothers, just as he believes the public lavatory in Amroth, locked the moment it was finished in case it was used, is with its tiling and its opulence the architectural wonder of his day.

Like Thomas Hardy's, his is not a large world. Though in his novels he may travel in time, it consists of where he was born and lived his life, so it provides him with his heroes and his villains, the latter being on the whole more numerous. You will probably not encounter anyone like him again, just as you will never read a book like this, written by a man who still had sufficient local knowledge to write it. So read on.

There was a village…

Byron Rogers

PEOPLE often ask why the church was built so far from the village, when they should really be asking why the village was built so far from the church. The simple answer is that the original village was in the area of the church, with a little shop at what is now known as the Norton, and which in earlier years had been known as Chantry Lane.

The inscription on the headstone of Jane Smith, who died in 1845 at the age of fifty-seven, says, 'Wife of Simon Smith of this village.'

The headstone of Jane Smith 'of this village'.

For generations the Smiths had farmed at Amroth Green. Long since overgrown, the remains of the house are still there in the wilderness on the left-hand side of the road coming down from the church, just inside the gate where the footpath leads to Eastlake. The house was on the site of the original Amroth Castle, about two hundred yards to the east of the church.

Apart from the hamlet in the area of Colby Lodge, originally known as Rhydlancoed, there were two other hamlets. There was Earwear,

The sluice on the course of the old leat from the Factory to the corn mill at Earwear.

with its mansion, which is now the Castle, with several cottages in the two adjoining valleys, and there was the New Inn. From mediaeval times, until as late as the 1860's, there was a thriving woollen and carding mill, known in its last years as the Factory, at Earwear, and the remains are still to be seen in the undergrowth, as is the course of the leat which brought the water down from below the woollen mill to power the Earwear corn mill at the bottom of the valley. Then there was the Burrows in the area of the Temple Bar.

Little now remains of the the hamlet of Rhydlancoed, most of the cottages having either been pulled down or allowed to fall down. Nearby was the 'Red Land Wig Colliery' worked by the Colbys in 1806-7. Shortly after its purchase in 1803, a large residence was built, the building of which was supervised by John Nash's Clerk of the Works, and named Colby Lodge after the then owners.

Colby Lodge.

According to Edward Laws, in his *Little England Beyond Wales*, it was from Colby Lodge that General Sir Thomas Picton left on his way to Waterloo, but there is no mention of what he would have been doing there.

At one time a private school, and then a Hydropathic Establishment, eventually it was bought by Samuel Kay, a Lancastrian industrial chemist, when it still seems to have been known as Rhydlangoed. Kay's daughter, Gladys, subsequently married Col. J.C.H. Crosland, who came to live there after the first World War. Although with a home in Cheshire, Mrs. Crosland devoted much of her life to the care of the gardens and woodland, with a particular love for her rhododendrons and azaleas.

When Mrs. Crosland died she left the estate to her niece, Miss Elidyr Mason, who bequeathed the bulk of it to the National Trust and sold the house and gardens to Mr. Ivo Chance, the Chairman of Christie's of London. This property, too, fell into the hands of the Trust after the Chance's days. Colby Lodge can be reached from the car park in the village along the public footpath, either direct to Colby Lodge, or via the Coombs to where there used to be a cottage at Brookside.

The oldest tombstone in the old churchyard was dated 1763. This was thought to have been made by Henry Rees at the Coombs. About that date Rees had established a local memorial stoneworks, with a circular stone saw driven by water power. A wheel from his long-since abandoned operation is still to be seen in the growth at the side of the footpath from the Coombs to Brookside, and the route of the leat which brought the water down to the Coombs is also still visible. This early example of harnessing power to cut down on

Iron wheel from Henry Rees's stoneworks at the Coombs.

manual labour led to a considerable reduction in the cost of gravestones, and it meant that headstones for the poor, as well as for the rich, now became the custom. There is a car park at Colby Lodge for those who prefer to pay to explore the grounds.

Originally there had been two ecclesiastical divisions. At Merrixton, on the west side, there is a piece of land which for centuries has been called the Church Field. There was also another small stone church, built on the east side of the parish, just inside and to the west of the present church entrance gate, which from being so near to his residence would seem to have been built by the lord of the old castle at Amroth Green. This castle was probably destroyed by Llewellyn during his devastating incursion of 1217-20 and, either through the owner's death

The Coombs, built in 1780, before it was restored in 1896

or departure from the district, his support and right of presentation to the little church on the east side lapsed. This was followed by further changes in the administration and adjustment of tithes, which resulted in the fixing of the parish boundary round the hitherto separated east and west wards, which then became united to form the ecclesiastical parish of Amroth. This boundary was adopted for Poor Law in 1601.

For many years the division of tithes between two churches in a single ecclesiastical parish caused confusion, especially with those who held land on both sides of the parish. The difficulty was further complicated through the glebeland income of the little church on the east side being appropriated by the Knights Hospitallers of St. John of Jerusalem, established at Slebech.

It was not until 1490 that any attempt was made to resolve the matter, when John Elliott of Earwear, in the days when the whole country was still Catholic, and who had already built his own chapel adjoining the mansion, recognised the objections of both sides to the possible disendowment of either one of the equally privileged little churches. He therefore initiated the proposal not to abolish either of the old churches, but to build instead one new larger church to serve the inhabitants both of east and west sides of the parish.

The stones for the building of the new church were available, practically on the spot, from the ruins of the old castle at Amroth Green. It is not known how much longer the church at Merrixton lasted, but the one on the east side was eventually restored and served as a day school until the building of a new school in 1859. Much earlier than that a school had been built by Squire Elliott at Earwear in 1713. It was provided with an

The only remaining visable evidence of the site of the old school.

income of £4 per year, as the result of the endeavours of Sir John Philipps, and the work of the Society for Promoting Christian Knowledge, and functioned until the early part of the 19th century. The only remaining visible evidence of it is where the beams can be seen to have been fitted into the wall just inside the archway at the entrance to the Castle drive.

Until comparatively recent times, the parish continued to be divided for parochial purposes into two embryo parishes. For the administration of the Poor Law under the system of the old Vestry Meetings, and later when the Parish Councils came into being, paupers on either side of the 'great divide' had to be supported by ratepayers living on that side of the stream which entered the sea at the Burrows. Overseers for the poor were always selected from either side of the parish. The Census Returns, too, after 1841, were taken separately east and west.

When the new church was built, the Chantry Chapel on the north side was built by John Elliott of Earwear for the chanting of Masses for the dead, in particular for himself and family who were to be buried in the vault there. In the event, Henry VIII decreed otherwise and abolished chantries.

In 1771, the old north door had been built up and a new door made on the south side. The gravel entrance walk, formerly situated on the north side of the tower, was made to pass round the south side, and the old stone kneeling steps outside were also removed from behind the tower to their present position near the main entrance out of respect to those Catholic parishioners who still clung to the belief that they, like their ancestors, should not fail to kneel at prayers on these steps before entering the church.

The Earwear estate was bought at the end of the 18th Century by Captain James Ackland, brother of Major Dudley Ackland of Boulston, of the 91st Regt. of Foot, a Lieutenant in the Pembrokeshire Yeomanry, who was one of the central figures in the Fishguard invasion. The Ackland family had lived in Warren Street in Tenby for some years. Ackland carried out vast structural alterations to the mansion, and its appearance would have been altered out of all recognition when its castellation gave rise to the name being changed to Amroth Castle. An interesting reference to the visit by Lord Nelson and Lady Hamilton, with a description of what Lady Hamilton wore, will be found in Mary Curtis's book, *The Antiquities of Laugharne, Pendine and their Neighbourhoods*. In spite of the many changes, much was to remain to give a fair idea of what the area of the chapel would have been like before Ackland's major alterations and additions.

In the east wall of the chapel there was a beautiful pre-Reformation stained glass window of the Crucifixion, depicting Our Lord, with His Blessed Mother, accompanied by John, weeping at the foot of the cross. This window was in perfect condition until 1960, but after the Castle was acquired by the late Fred Morgans, and planning permission had been condoned by the National Park for a huge caravan site, the chapel fell into a state of ruin and the window was vandalised.

Stone kneeling steps at St. Elidyr's.

Vandalised chapel window.

Part of Ackland's alterations included the sealing off of a tunnel, which led in the direction of the Mill or the beach, or possibly even the New Inn. It was rediscovered when the Castle was being established as a guesthouse in 1938, to a point at which there had been a fall after about forty or fifty yards. At the outbreak of war, when the Castle was requisitioned by the War Office, the military used outside buildings as latrines and turned the drain into the tunnel.

The purpose of the tunnel must remain a matter for conjecture, but two possible explanations present themselves. It must have had a purpose unconnected with mining, and the probability is that the tunnel was built to serve the needs of the smuggling trade, which was rife all along the coast until well into the 18th Century. Many of the gentry participated in it, but no doubt the tunnel would also have been used from time to time by those who came and went when Mass was still being offered in the years following the Reformation, when those who remained true to the Faith were highly suspect and under fierce suppression. It is equally certain that the Catholic Elliotts, who built the chapel, as well as being so concerned about, and involved with, work on the original Amroth Parish Church when it was still Catholic, would not lightly have turned, or been turned, from their Faith. Two hundred years after the arrival of the original John Elliott at Earwear, a descendant, John Eliot, who was a lawyer, was extremely active as an adviser and intriguer during the two Civil Wars of the 1640's.

Throughout the years that followed there is no record of who, if anybody, used the chapel for worship, but, in 1959, an approach was made by a Catholic priest, Fr. William Maram, a Travelling Missioner of the Redemptorists, who was seeking a place for the Catholics of the ecclesiastical parish, which included Saundersfoot, to say Mass. At that time there was no Catholic Church in Saundersfoot, and Mass was being offered in all sorts of unlikely places. Some of the nuns from Tenby turned up enthusiastically with buckets and mops, and did some white-liming to make the little sanctuary fit for worship once again. By 1960 Catholics were able to attend Mass in the newly opened Village Hall in Saundersfoot, until the new Catholic Church was built and eventually opened in 1966.

It would be interesting to know in how many pre-Reformation Churches anywhere in Wales the Mass has subsequently been offered, and this could possibly have been the first time for Mass to have been offered openly in a pre-Reformation Church since it had been proscribed centuries ago.

When Captain Ackland died he was buried in the south-west corner of the north aisle of Tenby's St. Mary's Church, and his widow was also buried there. The memorial plaque says, 'His cordial hospitality, inflexible integrity and spotless honour gained the esteem of all those to whom his person or

> Near this place are deposited the mortal remains of
> JAMES ACKLAND Esq! of Amroth Castle in this County
> who was born in 1749, and employed his early life in the Military
> service of his Country, with distinguished Gallantry and Humanity
> in 1787, he married FRANCES daughter of THO.S HANCORNE Esq
> and settled in this County where his cordial Hospitality
> inflexible Integrity and spotless Honor gained the esteem of
> all those to whom his Person or Character were known
> He departed this life the 10.th day of December 1820.
> deeply regretted by his numerous friends and by the Poor
> to whom he was a kind and liberal Benefactor.
>
> Also FRANCES his Widow who died at
> Amroth Castle March 8.th 1825.

Memorial plaque to James Ackland in St. Mary's church, Tenby.

character were known. He departed this life the 10th day of December 1820, deeply regretted by his numerous friends and by the poor, to whom he was a kind and liberal benefactor.' His widow, Frances, died at Amroth Castle, March 8th 1825.

Mention of his death is an opportune point to refer to the Castle Gate pit opposite the entrance to the Castle. This pit never worked, the sinking of it being abandoned when Ackland died suddenly. Such mining as there was in the parish had been carried out elsewhere many years previously. A full account can be found in M.R.C. Price's book, *Industrial Saundersfoot*. A visible reminder of the industrial life of the parish is still to be seen in the remains of the old lime kiln, possibly 17th Century or even earlier, in the paddock of the area which was once known as the Mead. In fact, time was when the whole area of what is now the village was known as the Mead.

The arch was the entrance to the Castle Gate pit which was abandoned before it could be worked. Immediately behind is the old Amroth Castle Arms which was demolished and replaced by the new house higher up. To the left is the old coast road where there is now a sea wall.

Remains of the old lime kiln.

Following Ackland's death the Earwear estate changed hands several times and, in the 1850's, the Castle was opened by a Dr. John Howard Norton as a private lunatic asylum. Full and fascinating details of Norton and how he operated are given in an article by Dr. T.G. Davies, a former consultant psychiatrist, in Vol. 5 of the *Journal of the Pembrokeshire Historical Society*. The whole exercise was a disastrous failure, although it took those who should have acted to protect the interests of the miserable patients the typically unconscionable length of time of officialdom to do anything. During one inspection it was found that a patient had been fastened to a fixed chair by a strap round her waist almost continuously for long periods and at times she had been placed in a straight waistcoat. There were numerous complaints about the inadequate food and the dark and gloomy accommodation. When the house was first visited by the Lunacy Commissioners in April 1852, they found two private and sixteen pauper patients there, twelve of whom had been taken from an asylum in Glamorgan.

The pauper patients were housed in the stable, which had been whitewashed and boarded, with few other structural alterations having been made. The house was closed in 1856, when Dr. Norton was still only in his mid-thirties. It can be seen from the Amroth Church burial registers that, during the five years of its operation as an asylum, at least sixteen patients died there with an average age of forty-six.

Norton left a permanent reminder of his time at Amroth with the name of Chantry Lane being changed to the Norton, at which it has now remained for a century-and-a-half.

A new chapter was opened in the history of what had once been Earwear when the estate was purchased in 1898 by Owen Cosby Philipps, scion of an old and propertied County family. A Liberal, he was elected to Parliament as Member for the Pembroke Boroughs in 1906, knighted in 1908, and created Lord Kylsant in 1923. His name will best be remembered for the fact that he was sentenced to twelve months in gaol in 1931 for his part in the publication of a misleading prospectus in his capacity as Chairman of the Royal Mail Steam Packet. His apologists, dwelling on the fact that he was indisputably a kind and upright man, and a good landlord, agreed with the claim in his defence that what he had done had been common practice insofar as he had failed to declare that dividends had been paid out of reserves rather than trading profits, and that he had acted in the interests of the shareholders and employees. Company Law had been altered in 1929 as a result of the events of the Kylsant prospectus, and it was stressed on behalf of the defence that what had been done in 1928 should not be regarded in the same light as when the case was now being heard three years later. It was also stressed that what had been done was common practice in the City at that time. During the prosperous years certain sums had been put to one side for a rainy day and, as a result, the company had been able to pay dividends out of savings when otherwise shareholders would have received nothing. Lord Kylsant was culpable insofar as he failed to point out that the dividends had been paid out of reserves and not out of trading profits. It was a fact, too, that he had appeared honestly to believe that, with the trading cycles which were typical of the business, there were better days ahead.

It is sad that his name is unlikely to be remembered for any of these things. The local people whose faith in him had been such that they had invested their life savings in his company, and lost everything, were more cognisant of the words of Mr. Justice Avory, who said when delivering the judgement of the Court of Criminal Appeal, that there was ample evidence on which the jury could find the prospectus was false in a material particular, and on which the jury could find that Lord Kylsant knew the falsity of the document.

For those who would know more of the intricate financial details of the case it is all there in the book, *The Royal Mail Case*, by John Collins, published by William Hodge & Co. (1933), as one of the volumes in their series, *Notable British Trials*. A number of so-called honourable gentlemen, including his brother Wynford, Viscount St. David's, had been privy to what was being done, and been more than ready to benefit from it, but were conveniently absent abroad when he stood in the dock alone.

The Kylsant era effectively ended when his daughter, Nesta Donne, married the Honourable George Coventry, of Croome Court in Worcestershire, and they came to live at Amroth Castle. It was a period which bequeathed many happy memories to the area, and an era which ended when the 9th Earl of Coventry, who had inherited the title from his grandfather in 1843, when only four years old, died in March 1930 at the age of ninety-two. His widow died three days later. Their son, George Coventry, became the 10th Earl, with the courtesy title Viscount Deerhurst, and he and his Countess moved back to the family home in Worcestershire.

A great sportsman, he participated in country pursuits with enthusiasm and gave the youths of the village a part of the Castle meadow for a football pitch. It was the start of the Amroth village football team, known as the Amroth Seagulls, of the 1920's. A boxer of considerable ability, he encouraged the village boys in the sport, and was not above calling them together in old-fashioned Corinthian style to settle their differences with the gloves on in the old laundry when they quarrelled.

In 1931 it was a measure of his sterling character that, not only was he in Court during every day of the Kylsant trial, but was

The 10th Earl of Coventry.

Amroth Seagulls.
Back row, left to right: Leslie Ebsworth; Harry Rees; Billy Philipps [Long Furze]; Stanley Irving; Willy Griffiths ['Satan']; Ben Lewis ['Clever Benny']
Front row, left to right: Lionel Isaac; Billy Phillips ['Nibloe']; Tom Ebsworth ['Tommy Dick']; Reggie Absalom; Roy Fletcher.

there to greet and accompany his father-in-law when Lord Kylsant was released from prison at the end of his sentence. The Earl of Coventry, as he had by then become, was killed during the first year of the war, and many of the older generation, not only in the Amroth area, felt a sense of great personal loss.

The Burrows was in the left foreground. Further along are the houses built from the 1850's onwards. To the right are the houses built in the 1880's and washed away in the 1930's, with Samuel Kay's boathouse in the right foreground.

When the Coventrys left, to general sadness in the area, in 1931, the Castle was let on a fully-repairing lease to the Ricketts, who spent very little time there. William Rickett, as a financier, was much in the news during the Abyssinian oil crisis in the 1930's, which, as the years passed, was responsible for the oft repeated silly story that Emperor Haile Selassie had stayed at Amroth Castle, when in fact he had never been near the place.

The hamlet known as the Burrows, in the area of the Temple Bar, was a cluster of maybe half-a-dozen cottages, built on the sandy soil of what would originally have been one of the Norman 'conygers', or burrows, for the breeding of rabbits, and from which the hamlet took its name. In 1841 only one dwelling was recorded under that name.

Although it is self-evident that the houses in the area of the Mead are modern, it is less easy to appreciate that the houses, plus Ebenezer chapel, from the Amroth Arms to the end of the row, have all been built within not much more than the last hundred years, as have most of the houses in the area of Beulah Hill and the Cliff Road. Henry Thomas, a renowned lay preacher of his day, who lived at the Burrows, built the house known as Beulah in 1857 in the area known as Stepshill. It was no doubt in keeping with the religious fervour of the day that it had become Beulah by 1891, having briefly been Beulah Hill...'*Oh Beulah Land, sweet Beulah Land, As on thy highest mount I stand, I look away across the sea...*'

Henry's son, James, who was injured in an accident, became a self-taught and very well-read scholar and, in an essay on the history of Amroth, with which he won the prize at the Amroth Big Day Eisteddfod in 1910, left behind a most valuable record, including an interesting reference to a former vicar of the parish.

The Rev. (afterwards Canon) W.D. Phillips, Rector of Crunwear from 1839-86, also became Vicar of Amroth in 1851. The Census shows him as living at Cliff Cottage in 1841. A powerful preacher, able politician and educationalist, he was revered by his parishioners, all of whom he visited regularly. Ever ready to assist them, he frequently used his great influence on their behalf when they were in legal difficulties. His contribution in helping to gain the reprieve of the unfortunate girl, Mary Prout, who had been condemned to death for having thrown her baby down a disused coal-pit in 1864, is a case in point.

Mary Curtis wrote of him, 'The Rev. Mr. Phillips is rector of Amroth, and holds Crunweir with it. He is much respected and beloved, preaches admirable sermons to crowded congregations.'

It is of interest that James Thomas had written of him, 'Prior to 1842, Canon Phillips resided at the Mead, Amroth, and in that year moved to the new Rectory at Crunwear, where he remained until his death on May 21st, 1886, aged 80 years. He was interred at Crunwear, where also his wife, Mrs. Henrietta Phillips – formerly an industrious Church worker – is interred.'

The interesting reference here is to Canon Phillips having lived at the Mead when, in fact, it is doubtful whether the house at the Mead had at that time been built. The whole area near the Burrows being known as the Mead, Cliff Cottage would have been included in that.

The first house to be built in the village row was at the eastern end of the village and was originally known as Albion House, built in the 1850's by Thomas Lewis, a mason, who also had a butcher's shop there. Up to that time the inn known as the Amroth Castle Arms was opposite the Castle entrance.

During the next fifty years, once these developments had begun, most of the building of what is now regarded as Amroth took place, with a row of five houses, known as Beach Cottages, being built on the sea side of

Cliff cottage.

Census Returns in 1891. In his recollections when he was an old man in 1923, Ben Price, who as a boy had worked at the Earwear corn mill for William Dalton, referred to the Thomas family of the Burrows and said, 'They provided nine tenths of the inhabitants of the Burrows sixty years ago. The three brothers, Thomas, William and John Thomas, occupied all the then existing houses except two, I think. There were no houses between the road and the beach, except the one under the cliff. I remember Mr. Thomas Thomas with much labour, forming a garden and beginning to grow vegetables between the road and the beach opposite the house in which he lived; and I remember Mr. Thomas Lewis building the first house between the bridge over the stream and the cottage opposite the Castle Gates.'

The Beach Cottages were built some time in the 1880's by John Richards, who was the son-in-law of Thomas Thomas, who had made the road opposite the Burrows, as well as along the area, from what had now become the Amroth Arms, to Albion House, and which for generations had sometimes been known as Croggans' Cliff, as well as the more correct Mead Cliff. It took the name Croggan from the nickname for the visitors who came from 'up the Welsh', on Amroth's traditional Big Day in August, which was where they assembled. The houses along Croggans' Cliff had gardens on the sea side of the road, but these gardens were washed away during the great storms of the 1890's.

Later, as well as the Beach Cottages where the sea wall and promenade now are, other houses were to be built in the village. Beach Cottages were entered for the first time in the

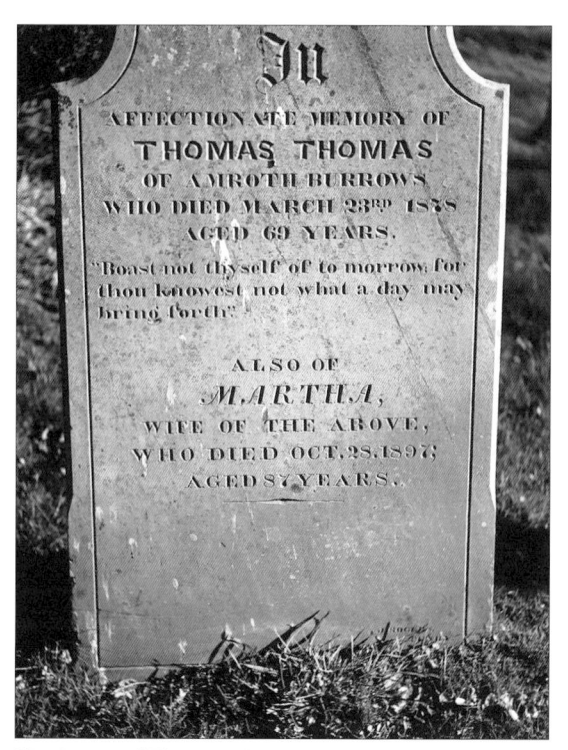

Headstone of Thomas Thomas.

the gardens there. They were eventually destroyed by the sea in the late 1930's. Although the name Earwear was falling into disuse by the turn of the century, and the name Amroth had come into being for the village by that time, the Burrows was still the name in use for the western end when today's older generation were children.

Ben Price's reference to the stream is interesting insofar as it goes some way to establishing when the change of course might have taken place. Tradition has it, and is almost certainly correct, that at one time the stream ran onto the beach in the area between Beach House, now known as Coedmôr, and Osborne Villa, now the site of Osborne Shop. At some time the stream changed its course to where it now runs, and it has been suggested that this happened following the great storms of 1896. This cannot be so, and it must have been long before that, because these two houses had been built before the end of the last century.

In addition to the houses along Croggans' Cliff, Ebenezer Chapel was built, in 1867, on land given by Benjamin Rees of Sunnyhill, who owned what was known as the Mead Estate. All the houses, including the new Amroth Arms, along the old Croggans' Cliff, were built on leasehold land belonging to the Mead Estate. Under post-war legislation the freeholds were acquired by the various leaseholders in the 1950's.

In the Picton Castle collection of papers in the National Library of Wales at Aberystwyth, there is a schedule of the valuation of houses at the Burrows end of the village when their ground rights were acquired from the Picton Estate in 1892 by Samuel Kay of Colby Lodge. Most of these leases, running for sixty years from some time in the 1860's, expired in the 1920's. In 1893 Kay also acquired other properties in the parish.

In 1882 when the cottage and holding known as Rook's Nest, on the old cliff road near Wisemansbridge, were sold, one lot also on offer was the valuable mineral rights, 'Coal and culm lying under Long Furze, Mead and Nathaniel's Meadow.' The accompanying map showed Nathaniel's Meadow as running up the valley towards the Coombs from where Brookside villas now are. Although the brook which runs through the village has no accepted name nowadays, time was when it was referred to as Brandy Lake, or sometimes the more alliterative Brandy Brook, because, in the Census Returns from 1861-'91 it stated, 'Part of the Parish of Amroth which is situated to the West (or East, as the case might be) of the Brook leading from Brandy Well to the sea.' In 1851 the reference had been to 'the stream of water that rises at Blaencilgoed in the parish of Ludchurch and discharges itself in the sea at the Burrows.'

If anything has ensured that Amroth has had more than its share of news headlines over the years, it has been the degree of coastal erosion, and the frequency with which the village has been battered by the sea during gales from the south and south-west. Much has been written on the sunken forest, and how the sea has been steadily encroaching, and Mary Curtis quoted conversations on the subject in the 1850's and '60's.

During the huge storm of 1896 part of the Castle garden wall was demolished, and pebbles were thrown up on to the coast road. In the age of the horse-and-cart and the wheelbarrow, before the advent of the drot and the JCB, it was out of the question to think of shifting such a huge bank of stones, and the road was simply remade on top of them. That layer of pebbles was come upon in the 1980's well below the surface of the present road, when the sewerage scheme was being carried out. It explains why the old archway, near the beach door, which was built up when Captain Ackland was making a new entrance, looks as if it would have been far too low to admit of the passage of a carriage.

The beach road after pebbles had been thrown up by the storms of the 1890's.

The bridge over the stream at New Inn was built in 1907 by Young Brothers of Maenchlochog. Until then there had been a ford, with a footbridge for those who walked, as shown in a picture taken in 1902. The Clerk of Works was a renowned stone-mason of his day, Alfred James, of Broomy Lake in the parish of Crunwear. His diary, in the possession of his grandson, Hugh James, himself a mason with the traditional craftsmanship of the family, records that Alfred James was paid the sum of £5 for his services by the Carmarthenshire and Pembrokeshire Highway Authorities, so that it was evidently a joint undertaking. He also turned the arch, which was work demanding considerable skill.

The ford at New Inn before the bridge was built. Beyond the Castle boundary wall the old Amroth Arms can be seen. The New Inn is in the foreground and Earwear Mill is between New Inn and the Castle.

After the bridge at New Inn had been built. The old Amroth Castle Arms and the archway to the Castle Gate pit have been demolished and the new gardener's house built.

At that time there was a boat-house which had been built at the Burrows by Samuel Kay, of Colby Lodge. It was on the sea side of the road, opposite to the Temple Bar, in the area where Thomas Thomas with much labour had formed a garden, and where his son-in-law, John Richards, had built the row of cottages between the road and the beach opposite the house in which they lived. That house, whilst being one of those entered in the various Census Returns merely as the Burrows, was to become one of the village shops and post

What remained of the Blackhorn caves before the storms of the 1890's.

office, which today is the shop of B.& J. Ceramics. The boat being kept in the boat-house in the autumn of 1896 was sucked out by the backwash of one of the great waves. What remained of it was washed up in many pieces, in spite of the great bank of pebbles, in the valley below the Factory. At the same time, much of what remained of the Blackhorn caves, by what is now known as Black Rock, was also destroyed during that historic storm. Following the destruction of the last of the caves a great arch had been left, which became known as Black Hall. One section was left standing to become known as the Pinnacle, but that was demolished during further storms in the 1920's.

One old Amroth native who, like so many of his generation, had needed to go 'up-line' to earn his living, was Dick Thomas of Dowlais. A brother of Jimmy Thomas, whose essay of 1910 was such a joy for those who would know something of the past, it would seem that the exile, too, had something of a way with words. The *Narberth Weekly News*, in its edition of November 18th, 1926, carried some verses by him.

Black Hall Arch, Amroth.

Historic Arch, alas, no more, hit hard by frost, by waves and storm,
Bright beauty spot on Amroth's shore, now battered, shapeless, rent and torn.
Old Neptune with terrific blows egged on by heartless Father Time,
Devoid of love, no mercy shows on mortal, landmark, arch or shrine.
To stately Arch we bid adieu, in minor strain its loss deplore.
For ever gone from human view, must now be classed with things of yore.
About two hundred years ago John Wesley passed on horse this way.
We think the Saint with mind aglow beheld this Arch and blessed the day.
Here Nelson gazed with pleasing eye, the antiquarian plied his pen,
The submerged forest green and dry grew food for prehistoric men.
Near by its base a thinker sat to write in book its hoary age.
"Two hundred years," instead of that please write ten thousand on its page.
Dear Editor of "Narberth News," keen lover of historic lore,
Insert these lines, imprint these views, and mourn with me for Amroth shore.

At the eastern end of what was now coming to be regarded as Amroth, as distinct from the houses by the Church, the gardens on the sea side of the road below Croggans' Cliff, from the Amroth Arms as far as Albion House, were almost completely washed away in 1896, leaving the road in a vulnerable state pending the next storms. The counter of the Amroth Arms was washed up against the back wall of the bar, and in the gardens of the Beach Cottages, householders' pigs had to be evacuated.

Although there appears to be no documentation on the subject, there must have been work done about that time by way of coast protection along the beach below Croggans' Cliff. Not far from Ebenezer chapel, on the opposite side of the road, there was a stable which had been built many years previously in conjunction with the work at the Patches, between Amroth and Wisemans-bridge, where for centuries iron ore had been extracted from the cliff, and it was in this stable that a couple of the horses were kept. The chapel had been built at about the time when work at Crickdam, the last of the Patches to be worked, was coming to an end, so the visiting preacher found ready-made stabling for his horse available on the spot. Access was by way of a track between the stables and the beach, but this fell victim to the sea along with the gardens in those storms of 1896.

It was following this that a certain amount of protection work must have been carried out, and the door and windows of the stable were built up. The bricks used for the lintels were from the brickworks at Templeton, which, according to Russell Morgan's *Jottings of Templeton and District* (1969), operated from some time in the 1880's to 1922. The bricks had the reputation of being unsuitable for outdoor work, but the name on each one, facing the worst that the elements can hurl at them on Amroth's exposed beach, still proudly gives the lie to that slander a century later.

The history of the Patches and of the tradition of Amroth Big Day can be found in *Old Saundersfoot, from Monkstone to Marros.*

In the years before the First World War a band was formed in the village, a canopy roof was built at road level above the stable, and it became known as the bandstand. The band, members of which bought their own instruments, was connected with the Band of Hope, but based at the Temple Bar, which possibly explains why it was not particularly well-supported, and its activities were short-lived. The bandstand, still known by that name, remained and a Mr Spry, a retired sailor with one arm, kept watch from there with a telescope during the war on the look-out for German submarines.

All this, if anything is needed to make the point, illustrates the eastward drift of the sea, driven by the prevailing wind, which is from the south-west, plus the fact that the flood tide coming up the Bristol Channel has much greater force than the ebb. Nowhere is the result of all this more evident than when taking note of the great bank of pebbles at the eastern end of the beach beyond New Inn, which was much greater at one time.

When steamships replaced the days of sail there was no longer any ballast to be jettisoned from coal boats entering Saundersfoot harbour. More crucially, with work at the Patches being abandoned in the 1870's, there was now no waste stone from that source being washed eastwards to replenish the existing stone which was also being washed eastwards. It is fascinating today to see lumps of ironstone amidst the pebbles, and to realise that it has taken maybe best part of a couple of centuries to wash them less than a mile along the beach. It is equally interesting to see how the pebbles are constantly being pulverised, as they are ground down smaller and smaller, eventually to become sand.

It would no doubt warrant a book in itself to chronicle all the episodes which have become part of the lore of storm and sea damage at Amroth, and not all of it has been confined to the autumn and winter months. In August, 1931, there was a storm on the night of Amroth's traditional Big Day concert, and much damage was done.

That would seem to have been a prelude to what was to come, because, in the November the storm damage was devastating and the road was closed. Pictures taken at the time show only too clearly that any hope of saving it would have been beyond the wit or means of those charged with that duty. The coast road was closed from Albion to the Castle entrance and diverted from the Amroth Arms to the Church, and down the private road which was once Chantry Lane, to rejoin the coast road at where the Castle green once was.

Eventually, at a meeting in May, 1932, the County Council agreed to abandon the old road and make a new one over the top of the hill at an estimated cost of £11,000, at the same time hoping for a grant from the Ministry which, up to that time, had been refused. In October it was reported at the Main

The storms of 1931 destroyed part of the coast road. A wall was built to replace it and a new road was made over the hill which necessitated demolishing the house in the background.

Roads Committee that the road was indeed being diverted inland, and, being on rock, 'would not be subject to damage from the sea.'

'What do you propose to do with the road that has been washed away?' asked Mr. William Davies, Tenby.

Sir Evan Jones, 'It is being diverted. Let the sea finish its work.'

At the end of June the Clerk was able to report that agreement with Lord Kylsant had been reached in the figure of £500. This was in respect of the gardener's house, which he had built when carrying out the demolition of the cottages originally known as the Amroth Castle Arms, and the area of land involved, which included a substantial part of the old Castle green. The Chairman was quoted as saying that he thought Lord Kylsant's offer was very fair. More than sixty years later there are still a few privets on the site where the house once stood, and a couple of apple trees which still bear fruit in season.

Whilst all the coast erosion in the early 1930's, and the need for protection at the eastern end of the village, had been the subject of much discussion and the usual procrastination by the County Council, there was even more havoc being wrought by the sea from time to time in the area of the Burrows.

About 1930 Thomas Richards had built six garages divided by wire-netting partitions. The garages, built opposite the Temple Bar on the site of Samuel Kay's former boat-house, were let to summer visitors at the rate of a shilling a night. At various times throughout the winter the partitions were removed and the garages eventually assumed the grandiose title of the Burrows Hall.

The scene of his operations was what had been entered variously over the years sometimes as the Burrows and sometimes as Beach Cottage, and he had also bought three of the old Burrows cottages and the land adjoining. He had inherited from his father, John Richards, who by 1881 had become established as the sub-postmaster. John had married Jane, the daughter of Thomas and Martha Thomas, and Thomas Thomas was the one who Ben Price remembered having 'with much labour, forming a garden and beginning to grow vegetables between the road and the beach opposite the house in which he lived'.

In due course Tommy Richards had also become, amongst other things, the Village postmaster. Concerned now for his own property, he realised the futility of waiting on Authority. The Highway Authority, in any case, having made it known that their road was not in danger, and that they would not protect private property, in desperation Thomas Richards built a wall at a cost of over £500. And that was in the early 1930's. It was to no avail. His wall, garages and the row of cottages had gone by the end of the decade.

In passing, it may be of interest that the Highway Authority did not take over the old Chantry Lane until 1938, when it was stated that the road from Amroth Arms to the Church, via Long Furze, would be de-classified.

Landing craft wrecked during *Jantzen* exercise, 1943.

An event which has been well chronicled, considering the degree of secrecy which was in force at the time, was the supply exercise in 1943, code-named *Jantzen*, prior to the Allies invasion of Normandy.

Before the *Jantzen* exercise, there had been another army presence when they came to lay anti-personnel mines in the bottom half of the field, known as Lawn Meadow, in front of the Castle, and it was enclosed by barbed wire. The officer-in-charge explained that each mine was connected to the next one by wire,

Burrows cottages left foreground. Beach cottages on right. c. 1910.

The storms of 1931.
The garages and Burrows Hall on right with Thomas Richards' wall on extreme right. Cliff Cottage in right foreground and Burrows cottages in left foreground.

so that, when the time came to remove the mines, it would only be necessary to locate the first mine with a mine detector, and then the wire would lead to the next mine and so on until they were all located and removed.

The mines were laid when the first threat of invasion had passed. When there was again a threat of invasion it was decided to remove them, and the first mine was detected without any trouble. It was then discovered, however, that the connecting wire had rusted, so that every mine had to be located individually. A map had been supplied to the occupier showing that fifty-three mines had been laid. Now, an apologetic officer admitted that they could locate only fifty-one, and there the matter was left. Nobody could say for sure whether the original plan had been correct, or whether there were two recalcitrant mines which had refused to be located. Eventually the cows were turned into the previously wired-off area of the mine-field, and there was no mishap. That was more than fifty years ago and there has been no mishap since, so it is safe enough to assume by now that everything is all right. If they are still there, let us hope that they are under one of the caravans so that nobody can tread on them.

Part of the *Jantzen* exercise involved the eastern end of the beach at Amroth, where there was a huge disturbance of the stones by bull-dozers in levelling them off and making seven roadways up the beach to enable the various landing craft to come ashore. The inlets created for the landing craft to nuzzle into also gave the sea finger-holds to grasp at the storm beach of pebbles and tear massive amounts eastwards.

One of the vehicle-carrying landing craft was wrecked opposite the Castle entrance, and for a few years its iron frame remained, before it finally sank into the sand. In 1946, an old school-days friend of mine, Collin Bowen, who was born in Narberth, had just returned from the war in which he had had some experience as a staff officer and was familiar with the concept of making an 'appreciation' of a situation which demanded urgent action, and he interested himself in what had been done to the beach. His father had a bungalow at Wisemansbridge, so, apart from any question of scholarship, Collin had some practical knowledge of the area. He had staying with him at the time a former army colleague, Major (later Professor) F.G. ('Hank') Hannell, a senior lecturer in the Department of Geography at Bristol University, who joined him in, and advised on, the 'appreciation'.

On making enquiries, he was told by a fellow army officer, who had been involved in exercise *Jantzen*, that not only had thousands of tons of stones been shifted, but many loads had been driven away to make hard standings at nearby Marros Mountain.

Collin Bowen then wrote a report of the position as he saw it and took pictures to illustrate the points he was making. The disturbance of the stones had exacerbated the natural drift towards the east, and he suggested that, as a short-term measure, shingle should be carried back from the useless pile at the east to make good some of the deficiencies at the places to the west from which they had been moved. Initially, he suggested that the Army should mount its own operation for this purpose. Although no attempt was made to do this at the time, now, more than fifty years later, it is being done as part of the scheme currently being tackled in stages. Another of his suggestions was to import tons of stones as a temporary measure until a more comprehensive scheme could be undertaken.

When some thousands of pounds had subsequently been extracted from the War Department as a result of Collin Bowen's initiative, hundreds of loads of stones were driven from Gellyhalog quarry as a temporary measure. They served their purpose for a time and, in the 1950's, a scheme was embarked on which eventually included the building of sea walls opposite the Castle and the village, as well as a wall where the Roads and Bridges Committee had once been told that the sea could be left to do its work, for it had well and truly done so. There were also groins to check the drift of pebbles in their constant movement towards the east. Two hundred years ago, Captain Ackland, as related in *Old Saundersfoot, from Monkstone to Marros*, did a great deal of work in the 1790's laying pitching stones along the beach in front of the Castle, and from time to time after rough seas traces can still be seen.

Traces of Captain Ackland's pitching stones.

Of some small interest to the industrial archaeologist could be the fact that the stanchions for the series of groins were rails from the old Maenchlochog railway track, which was lifted in 1952, the story of which is told in *'The Maenchlochog Railway'* (1992), by John Gale.

When the row of cottages in the village had been demolished in the 1930's, the ruins of Cliff Cottage remained. When the new wall and promenade were built, what was left of Cliff Cottage had to go, and a public convenience was eventually built on the site. Before that, most of the stones from the old house had been used for the foundations of the Village Hall, which was opened in time for the Coronation celebrations in 1953, and demolished in the 1980's to be replaced by what is known as an enhancement area. But more of that and the palatial new public convenience another day.

Rails from Maenclochog Railway used for sea-defences.